Zuggy the Pug – Adoption Day
Written by Jean Marie Alfieri
Illustrations by Alexandra Ruiz
Graphic Design and Layout by Christine Sterling-Bortner

Copyright 2020 All rights reserved.

No part of this story or book may be reproduced, stored in a retrieval system, or transmitted in any form or by any means, electronic, mechanical, copying, recording, or otherwise, without the written permission of the author.
Printed in the U.S.A.

All Rights Reserved   First Edition

Dedication

To the volunteers, staff, and supporters of rescue shelters worldwide, for providing homeless animals a second chance at life. ~ JMA

To my mom Nerissa, my brother Nikolai, my sister Natasha, and to my friends for their never-ending support. And to the wonderful people who rescue and adopt animals, giving them the home and love they deserve. ~ AR

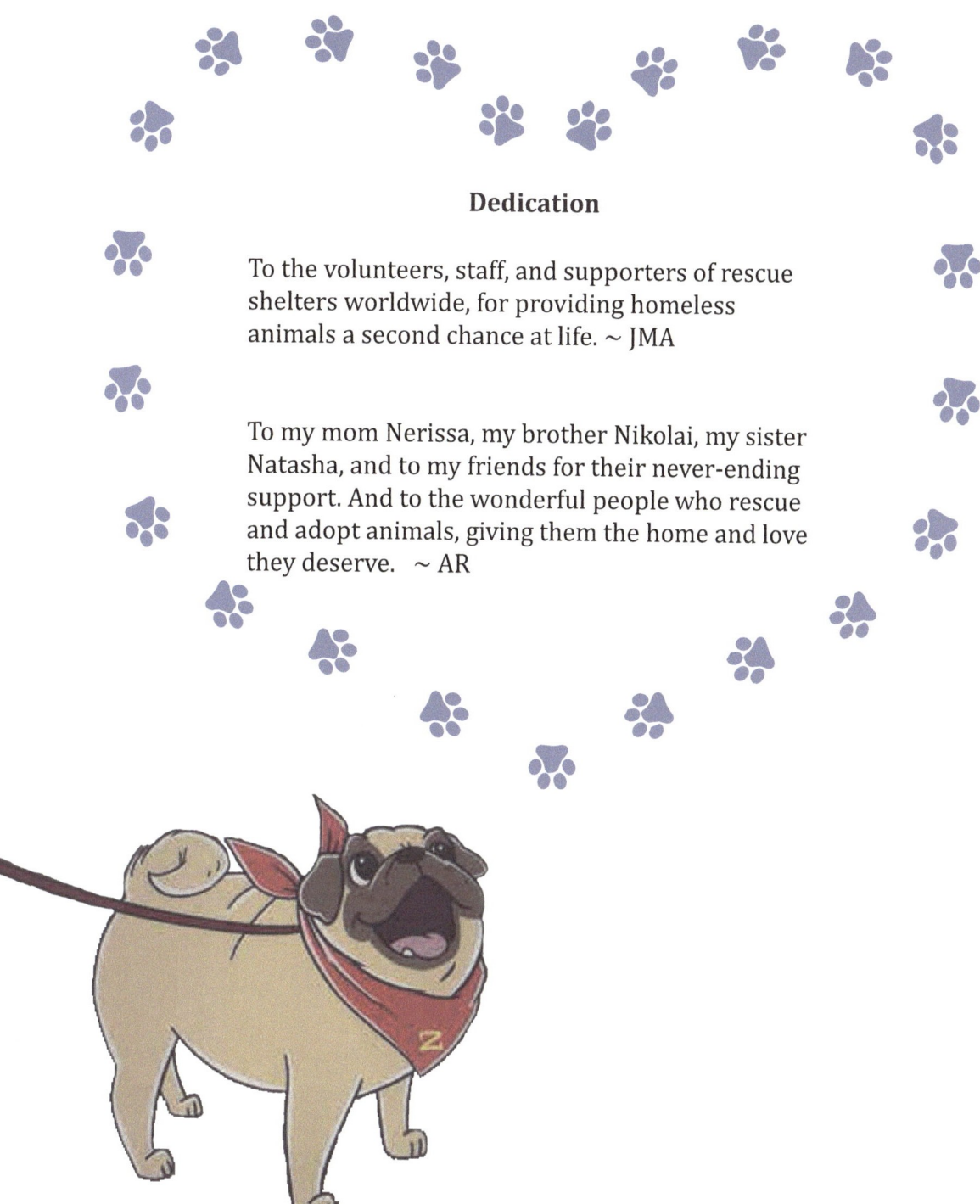

I'm Zuggy the Pug
And this is the tale,
Of those who helped me,
When alone I would fail.

They say that my Mom
Was a neighborhood stray.
She had a small litter
And then ran away.

We lived under a porch
And snuck out by day.
We rummaged for food.
In the dirt we would lay.

Cold, dark and musty,
Sometimes it was scary.
We lived with big rats
And spiders all hairy.

We snuggled together,
But still it was tough.
Avoiding coyotes
Was especially rough.

Then one afternoon,
While napping like cats,
We were startled awake
By the crack of a bat.

A baseball rolled in.
We heard, "Where'd it go?"
A girl peeked at us.
Her voice whispered, "Whoa."

"Hey fellas, come here!"
We heard them trot over.
She was pulling us out
Into the soft clover.

"Look what I found,"
Janie started to say.
Stopped dead in their tracks,
Jeff and Josh said, "No way!"

I rolled in the grass
As she petted my head.
"You will be alright.
We'll see that you're fed."

They gathered us up.
Janie knew what to do.
She said we'd be alright.
I hoped it was true.

We went to the place
Where she volunteers.
"Oh my," said the lady,
"What cute little dears!"

After being checked in,
More people met us.
With smiles and scratches,
They made quite a fuss!

I got a warm bath.
So good to be clean.
This shelter was nice.
And no one was mean.

After my check-up,
The vet had concerns.
"I'm ordering meds.
This pug-dog has worms.

He can't be adopted
Until he gets better."
Behind me was waiting
A young Irish Setter.

"What is 'adopted'?"
I asked the big pup.
"Just got here," he shrugged.
"Can't tell ya what's up."

Into my food bowl
A powder was sprinkled.
Then I got a long walk
So I could go tinkle.

They said I was thin.
I soon gained a tad.
My next check-up was good.
My belly was glad!

"He's healthy and well,"
Reported the vet.
"Ready for adoption."
She gave me a pet.

"What is adoption?"
I tilted my head.
There wasn't an answer,
But a biscuit instead!

Next, it was time
For my photo-shoot.
I worked the runway
And tried to look cute!

I posed for the pictures
With a squeaky red ball.
Then saw my sister
As we passed in the hall.

"Where are you going?"
I quickly asked her.
"I'm getting adopted.
It's finally my turn!"

"What is adopted?
I really must know!"
"You'll find out," she promised,
"But now I must go!"

I sat on my blanket.
This place was so great.
But I wanted a home.
How long would I wait?

Some people looked in.
Some others walked by.
Not even one visit.
I wanted to cry.

I started to worry,
"Did no one want me?
I'm such a great dog!
Can't anyone see?"

I found out later,
That right down the road
A family's dog had just died,
Who was very old.

It made them so sad.
But they were ready to get
A handsome young dog
To be their new pet.

My picture was posted,
Then a boy named Roy
Came with his sister,
And brought me a toy.

"Sorry for your loss,"
I heard Janie say.
Roy nodded and said,
"Thanks. We're doing okay."

Janie introduced us.
We played for a while.
"Want to be adopted?"
Roy asked with a smile.

I gave him a lick.
"I'm sure that I do!
If it means that I get
To go home with you!"

"I think that he does,"
Said Roy's sister, Pearl.
I spun in a circle
And did a quick twirl.

I got loved and cared for,
In so many ways,
But finding my new home
Was the best part of my stay.

I'll always be thankful
For those who helped me.
In my fur-ever home,
I'm happy to be!

The End

ABOUT THE POET AND HER PUG

A wanderer at heart, Jean was born and raised outside of Chicago, Illinois. She currently resides in Colorado Springs, Colorado. But if home is where your heart is, for Jean, that would be Milwaukee, Wisconsin (in the summer). And in the winter, it would be her "desert home" of Phoenix, Arizona.

Regardless of her residence, as long as Jean has her loving husband, her precious pug, and a pen and paper in hand, she is happy!

Visit the photo gallery at: www.ZuggythePug.com

Want more Zuggy?

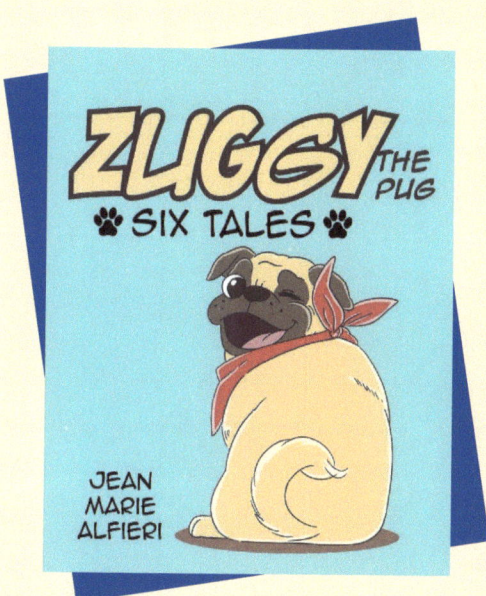

Zuggy the Pug - Six Tales

Check out these two Zuggy books available on Amazon! Get your copy (Paperback or Kindle) today!

Zuggy the Pug –
Four on the Floor

And remember to visit us at ZuggyThePug.com!

www.ingramcontent.com/pod-product-compliance
Lightning Source LLC
Chambersburg PA
CBHW042129040426
42450CB00002B/131